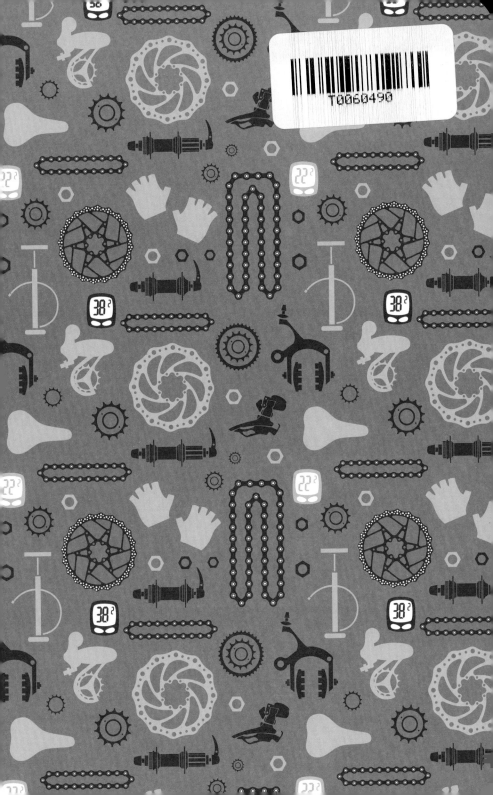

THIS JOURNAL BELONGS TO

_____

THE
CYCLIST'S JOURNAL

HOW TO USE THIS BOOK

WELCOME TO YOUR JOURNAL, a place to reflect on your cycling experiences, track your progress, and preserve memories of your most glorious rides.

This journal is divided into three parts. The first, Cycling Logs, is the heart of the book. Here, you can record details about every time you go biking, map out and describe your favorite routes, and note any unusual sights you saw along the way. Each log has a page with blank spaces for key information about the route, the weather, your distance and speed, plus a lined page for observations and additional notes. At the beginning of the section, you'll find a DIY index where you can enter the location and date for each log entry as you work through the journal.

Following the logs, the Notes & Sketches section features lined and blank pages where you can draw maps or sketches, update your equipment lists, track a training regimen, or just reminisce about a great day on the trail.

The final section, Cycling Checklists, gives you a place to list your favorite trips, your cycling bucket list, the gear you think is essential, your most challenging rides, and all the amazing sights you've seen on your rides so far.

HAPPY CYCLING!

CYCLING LOGS

CYCLING LOG INDEX

LOG #	LOCATION	DATE

LOG #	LOCATION	DATE

CYCLING LOG INDEX

LOG #	LOCATION	DATE

LOG #	LOCATION	DATE

CYCLING LOG

LOG #

DATE

START TIME

END TIME

LOCATION

OBSERVATIONS

WEATHER _____

ROUTE _____
_____
_____
_____

DISTANCE _____

ELEVATION (gain/loss) _____

AVERAGE SPEED _____

DIFFICULTY	1	2	3	4	5	6	7	8	9	10

TERRAIN NOTES _____
_____
_____

EQUIPMENT NOTES _____
_____
_____

HIGHLIGHTS _____
_____
_____
_____
_____

OVERALL RATING ⚙ ⚙ ⚙ ⚙ ⚙

CYCLING LOG

LOG #

DATE

START TIME

END TIME

LOCATION

OBSERVATIONS

WEATHER _____

ROUTE _____

_____

_____

_____

DISTANCE _____

ELEVATION (gain/loss) _____

AVERAGE SPEED _____

| DIFFICULTY | 1 | 2 | 3 | 4 | 5 | 6 | 7 | 8 | 9 | 10 |

TERRAIN NOTES _____

_____

_____

EQUIPMENT NOTES _____

_____

_____

HIGHLIGHTS _____

_____

_____

_____

OVERALL RATING ✿ ✿ ✿ ✿ ✿

CYCLING LOG

LOG #

DATE

START TIME

END TIME

LOCATION

OBSERVATIONS

WEATHER _____

ROUTE _____

_____

_____

_____

DISTANCE _____

ELEVATION (gain/loss) _____

AVERAGE SPEED _____

DIFFICULTY	1	2	3	4	5	6	7	8	9	10

TERRAIN NOTES _____

_____

_____

EQUIPMENT NOTES _____

_____

_____

HIGHLIGHTS _____

_____

_____

_____

_____

OVERALL RATING ✿ ✿ ✿ ✿ ✿

CYCLING LOG

LOG #

DATE	START TIME	END TIME

LOCATION

OBSERVATIONS

WEATHER _____

ROUTE _____

_____

_____

_____

DISTANCE _____

ELEVATION (gain/loss) _____

AVERAGE SPEED _____

| DIFFICULTY | 1 | 2 | 3 | 4 | 5 | 6 | 7 | 8 | 9 | 10 |

TERRAIN NOTES _____

_____

_____

EQUIPMENT NOTES _____

_____

_____

HIGHLIGHTS _____

_____

_____

_____

OVERALL RATING ✿ ✿ ✿ ✿ ✿

CYCLING LOG

LOG #

DATE

START TIME

END TIME

LOCATION

OBSERVATIONS

WEATHER _____

ROUTE _____

_____

_____

_____

DISTANCE _____

ELEVATION (gain/loss) _____

AVERAGE SPEED _____

DIFFICULTY   1   2   3   4   5   6   7   8   9   10

TERRAIN NOTES _____

_____

_____

EQUIPMENT NOTES _____

_____

_____

HIGHLIGHTS _____

_____

_____

_____

_____

OVERALL RATING ⚙ ⚙ ⚙ ⚙ ⚙

CYCLING LOG

LOG #

DATE

START TIME

END TIME

LOCATION

OBSERVATIONS

WEATHER _____

ROUTE _____

_____

_____

_____

DISTANCE _____

ELEVATION (gain/loss) _____

AVERAGE SPEED _____

DIFFICULTY	1	2	3	4	5	6	7	8	9	10

TERRAIN NOTES _____

_____

_____

EQUIPMENT NOTES _____

_____

_____

HIGHLIGHTS _____

_____

_____

_____

OVERALL RATING

CYCLING LOG

LOG #

DATE

START TIME

END TIME

LOCATION

OBSERVATIONS

WEATHER _____

ROUTE _____

_____

_____

_____

DISTANCE _____

ELEVATION (gain/loss) _____

AVERAGE SPEED _____

DIFFICULTY	1	2	3	4	5	6	7	8	9	10

TERRAIN NOTES _____

_____

_____

EQUIPMENT NOTES _____

_____

_____

HIGHLIGHTS _____

_____

_____

_____

_____

OVERALL RATING

CYCLING LOG

LOG #

DATE

START TIME

END TIME

LOCATION

OBSERVATIONS

WEATHER _____

ROUTE _____

_____

_____

_____

DISTANCE _____

ELEVATION (gain/loss) _____

AVERAGE SPEED _____

DIFFICULTY	1	2	3	4	5	6	7	8	9	10

TERRAIN NOTES _____

_____

_____

EQUIPMENT NOTES _____

_____

_____

HIGHLIGHTS _____

_____

_____

_____

_____

OVERALL RATING ✿ ✿ ✿ ✿ ✿

CYCLING LOG

LOG #

DATE

START TIME

END TIME

LOCATION

OBSERVATIONS

WEATHER _____

ROUTE _____
_____
_____
_____

DISTANCE _____

ELEVATION (gain/loss) _____

AVERAGE SPEED _____

DIFFICULTY	1	2	3	4	5	6	7	8	9	10

TERRAIN NOTES _____
_____
_____

EQUIPMENT NOTES _____
_____
_____

HIGHLIGHTS _____
_____
_____
_____

OVERALL RATING

CYCLING LOG

LOG #

DATE

START TIME

END TIME

LOCATION

OBSERVATIONS

WEATHER

ROUTE

DISTANCE

ELEVATION (gain/loss)

AVERAGE SPEED

DIFFICULTY	1	2	3	4	5	6	7	8	9	10

TERRAIN NOTES

EQUIPMENT NOTES

HIGHLIGHTS

OVERALL RATING ⚙ ⚙ ⚙ ⚙ ⚙

CYCLING LOG

LOG #

DATE	START TIME	END TIME

LOCATION

OBSERVATIONS

WEATHER _____

ROUTE _____
_____
_____
_____

DISTANCE _____

ELEVATION (gain/loss) _____

AVERAGE SPEED _____

DIFFICULTY	1	2	3	4	5	6	7	8	9	10

TERRAIN NOTES _____
_____
_____

EQUIPMENT NOTES _____
_____
_____

HIGHLIGHTS _____
_____
_____
_____

OVERALL RATING ⚙ ⚙ ⚙ ⚙ ⚙

CYCLING LOG

LOG #

DATE

START TIME

END TIME

LOCATION

OBSERVATIONS

WEATHER _____

ROUTE _____
_____
_____
_____

DISTANCE _____

ELEVATION (gain/loss) _____

AVERAGE SPEED _____

DIFFICULTY	1	2	3	4	5	6	7	8	9	10

TERRAIN NOTES _____
_____
_____

EQUIPMENT NOTES _____
_____
_____

HIGHLIGHTS _____
_____
_____
_____
_____

OVERALL RATING

CYCLING LOG

LOG #

DATE

START TIME

END TIME

LOCATION

OBSERVATIONS

WEATHER _____

ROUTE _____

_____

_____

_____

DISTANCE _____

ELEVATION (gain/loss) _____

AVERAGE SPEED _____

DIFFICULTY	1	2	3	4	5	6	7	8	9	10

TERRAIN NOTES _____

_____

_____

EQUIPMENT NOTES _____

_____

_____

HIGHLIGHTS _____

_____

_____

_____

OVERALL RATING ✿ ✿ ✿ ✿ ✿

CYCLING LOG

LOG #

DATE

START TIME

END TIME

LOCATION

OBSERVATIONS

WEATHER _____

ROUTE _____
_____
_____
_____

DISTANCE _____

ELEVATION (gain/loss) _____

AVERAGE SPEED _____

DIFFICULTY	1	2	3	4	5	6	7	8	9	10

TERRAIN NOTES _____
_____
_____

EQUIPMENT NOTES _____
_____
_____

HIGHLIGHTS _____
_____
_____
_____

OVERALL RATING ⚙ ⚙ ⚙ ⚙ ⚙

CYCLING LOG

LOG #

DATE

START TIME

END TIME

LOCATION

OBSERVATIONS

WEATHER _____

ROUTE _____
_____
_____
_____

DISTANCE _____

ELEVATION (gain/loss) _____

AVERAGE SPEED _____

DIFFICULTY 1   2   3   4   5   6   7   8   9   10

TERRAIN NOTES _____
_____
_____

EQUIPMENT NOTES _____
_____
_____

HIGHLIGHTS _____
_____
_____
_____

OVERALL RATING ✹ ✹ ✹ ✹ ✹

CYCLING LOG

LOG #

DATE

START TIME

END TIME

LOCATION

OBSERVATIONS

WEATHER _____

ROUTE _____

_____

_____

_____

DISTANCE _____

ELEVATION (gain/loss) _____

AVERAGE SPEED _____

DIFFICULTY	1	2	3	4	5	6	7	8	9	10

TERRAIN NOTES _____

_____

_____

EQUIPMENT NOTES _____

_____

_____

HIGHLIGHTS _____

_____

_____

_____

_____

OVERALL RATING ⚙ ⚙ ⚙ ⚙ ⚙

CYCLING LOG

LOG #

DATE

START TIME

END TIME

LOCATION

OBSERVATIONS

WEATHER _____

ROUTE _____

_____

_____

_____

DISTANCE _____

ELEVATION (gain/loss) _____

AVERAGE SPEED _____

DIFFICULTY	1	2	3	4	5	6	7	8	9	10

TERRAIN NOTES _____

_____

_____

EQUIPMENT NOTES _____

_____

_____

HIGHLIGHTS _____

_____

_____

_____

_____

OVERALL RATING ⚙ ⚙ ⚙ ⚙ ⚙

CYCLING LOG

LOG #

| DATE | START TIME | END TIME |

LOCATION

OBSERVATIONS

WEATHER

ROUTE

DISTANCE

ELEVATION (gain/loss)

AVERAGE SPEED

DIFFICULTY   1   2   3   4   5   6   7   8   9   10

TERRAIN NOTES

EQUIPMENT NOTES

HIGHLIGHTS

OVERALL RATING

CYCLING LOG

LOG #

DATE

START TIME

END TIME

LOCATION

OBSERVATIONS

WEATHER _____

ROUTE _____
_____
_____
_____

DISTANCE _____

ELEVATION (gain/loss) _____

AVERAGE SPEED _____

DIFFICULTY   1   2   3   4   5   6   7   8   9   10

TERRAIN NOTES _____
_____
_____

EQUIPMENT NOTES _____
_____
_____

HIGHLIGHTS _____
_____
_____
_____

OVERALL RATING ✿ ✿ ✿ ✿ ✿

CYCLING LOG

LOG #

DATE

START TIME

END TIME

LOCATION

OBSERVATIONS

WEATHER

ROUTE

DISTANCE

ELEVATION (gain/loss)

AVERAGE SPEED

DIFFICULTY	1	2	3	4	5	6	7	8	9	10

TERRAIN NOTES

EQUIPMENT NOTES

HIGHLIGHTS

OVERALL RATING

CYCLING LOG

LOG #

DATE

START TIME

END TIME

LOCATION

OBSERVATIONS

WEATHER _____

ROUTE _____
_____
_____
_____

DISTANCE _____

ELEVATION (gain/loss) _____

AVERAGE SPEED _____

DIFFICULTY 1 2 3 4 5 6 7 8 9 10

TERRAIN NOTES _____
_____
_____

EQUIPMENT NOTES _____
_____
_____

HIGHLIGHTS _____
_____
_____
_____

OVERALL RATING ⚙ ⚙ ⚙ ⚙ ⚙

CYCLING LOG

LOG #

DATE

START TIME

END TIME

LOCATION

OBSERVATIONS

WEATHER _____

ROUTE _____
_____
_____
_____

DISTANCE _____

ELEVATION (gain/loss) _____

AVERAGE SPEED _____

DIFFICULTY	1	2	3	4	5	6	7	8	9	10

TERRAIN NOTES _____
_____
_____

EQUIPMENT NOTES _____
_____
_____

HIGHLIGHTS _____
_____
_____
_____

OVERALL RATING ✿ ✿ ✿ ✿ ✿

CYCLING LOG

LOG #

DATE

START TIME

END TIME

LOCATION

OBSERVATIONS

WEATHER _____

ROUTE _____
_____
_____
_____

DISTANCE _____

ELEVATION (gain/loss) _____

AVERAGE SPEED _____

DIFFICULTY   1   2   3   4   5   6   7   8   9   10

TERRAIN NOTES _____
_____
_____

EQUIPMENT NOTES _____
_____
_____

HIGHLIGHTS _____
_____
_____
_____

OVERALL RATING   ⚙ ⚙ ⚙ ⚙ ⚙

CYCLING LOG

DATE

START TIME

END TIME

LOCATION

OBSERVATIONS

WEATHER _____

ROUTE _____

_____

_____

_____

DISTANCE _____

ELEVATION (gain/loss) _____

AVERAGE SPEED _____

DIFFICULTY   1   2   3   4   5   6   7   8   9   10

TERRAIN NOTES _____

_____

_____

EQUIPMENT NOTES _____

_____

_____

HIGHLIGHTS _____

_____

_____

_____

OVERALL RATING ✿ ✿ ✿ ✿ ✿

CYCLING LOG

LOG #

DATE

START TIME

END TIME

LOCATION

OBSERVATIONS

WEATHER _____

ROUTE _____

_____

_____

_____

DISTANCE _____

ELEVATION (gain/loss) _____

AVERAGE SPEED _____

DIFFICULTY	1	2	3	4	5	6	7	8	9	10

TERRAIN NOTES _____

_____

_____

EQUIPMENT NOTES _____

_____

_____

HIGHLIGHTS _____

_____

_____

_____

OVERALL RATING   ✿ ✿ ✿ ✿ ✿

CYCLING LOG

LOG #

DATE	START TIME	END TIME

LOCATION

OBSERVATIONS _____

WEATHER _____

ROUTE _____

_____

_____

_____

DISTANCE _____

ELEVATION (gain/loss) _____

AVERAGE SPEED _____

DIFFICULTY	1	2	3	4	5	6	7	8	9	10

TERRAIN NOTES _____

_____

_____

EQUIPMENT NOTES _____

_____

_____

HIGHLIGHTS _____

_____

_____

_____

_____

OVERALL RATING ⚙ ⚙ ⚙ ⚙ ⚙

CYCLING LOG

LOG #

DATE

START TIME

END TIME

LOCATION

OBSERVATIONS

WEATHER

ROUTE

DISTANCE

ELEVATION (gain/loss)

AVERAGE SPEED

DIFFICULTY   1   2   3   4   5   6   7   8   9   10

TERRAIN NOTES

EQUIPMENT NOTES

HIGHLIGHTS

OVERALL RATING

CYCLING LOG

LOG #

DATE	START TIME	END TIME

LOCATION

OBSERVATIONS

WEATHER _____

ROUTE _____

_____

_____

_____

DISTANCE _____

ELEVATION (gain/loss) _____

AVERAGE SPEED _____

DIFFICULTY	1	2	3	4	5	6	7	8	9	10

TERRAIN NOTES _____

_____

_____

EQUIPMENT NOTES _____

_____

_____

HIGHLIGHTS _____

_____

_____

_____

_____

OVERALL RATING ⚙ ⚙ ⚙ ⚙ ⚙

CYCLING LOG

LOG #

DATE

START TIME

END TIME

LOCATION

OBSERVATIONS

WEATHER

ROUTE

DISTANCE

ELEVATION (gain/loss)

AVERAGE SPEED

DIFFICULTY	1	2	3	4	5	6	7	8	9	10

TERRAIN NOTES

EQUIPMENT NOTES

HIGHLIGHTS

OVERALL RATING

CYCLING LOG

LOG #

DATE	START TIME	END TIME

LOCATION

OBSERVATIONS

WEATHER _____

ROUTE _____

_____

_____

_____

DISTANCE _____

ELEVATION (gain/loss) _____

AVERAGE SPEED _____

DIFFICULTY	1	2	3	4	5	6	7	8	9	10

TERRAIN NOTES _____

_____

_____

EQUIPMENT NOTES _____

_____

_____

HIGHLIGHTS _____

_____

_____

_____

OVERALL RATING

CYCLING LOG

LOG #

DATE

START TIME

END TIME

LOCATION

OBSERVATIONS

WEATHER _____

ROUTE _____

_____

_____

_____

DISTANCE _____

ELEVATION (gain/loss) _____

AVERAGE SPEED _____

DIFFICULTY	1	2	3	4	5	6	7	8	9	10

TERRAIN NOTES _____

_____

_____

EQUIPMENT NOTES _____

_____

_____

HIGHLIGHTS _____

_____

_____

_____

_____

OVERALL RATING ⚙ ⚙ ⚙ ⚙ ⚙

CYCLING LOG

LOG #

DATE

START TIME

END TIME

LOCATION

OBSERVATIONS

WEATHER _____

ROUTE _____
_____
_____
_____

DISTANCE _____

ELEVATION (gain/loss) _____

AVERAGE SPEED _____

DIFFICULTY	1	2	3	4	5	6	7	8	9	10

TERRAIN NOTES _____
_____
_____

EQUIPMENT NOTES _____
_____
_____

HIGHLIGHTS _____
_____
_____
_____

OVERALL RATING ⚙ ⚙ ⚙ ⚙ ⚙

CYCLING LOG

LOG #

DATE

START TIME

END TIME

LOCATION

OBSERVATIONS

WEATHER _____

ROUTE _____
_____
_____
_____

DISTANCE _____

ELEVATION (gain/loss) _____

AVERAGE SPEED _____

DIFFICULTY	1	2	3	4	5	6	7	8	9	10

TERRAIN NOTES _____
_____
_____

EQUIPMENT NOTES _____
_____
_____

HIGHLIGHTS _____
_____
_____
_____

OVERALL RATING ⚙ ⚙ ⚙ ⚙ ⚙

CYCLING LOG

LOG #

DATE

START TIME

END TIME

LOCATION

OBSERVATIONS

WEATHER _____

ROUTE _____

_____

_____

_____

DISTANCE _____

ELEVATION (gain/loss) _____

AVERAGE SPEED _____

DIFFICULTY   1   2   3   4   5   6   7   8   9   10

TERRAIN NOTES _____

_____

_____

EQUIPMENT NOTES _____

_____

_____

HIGHLIGHTS _____

_____

_____

_____

OVERALL RATING   ✿ ✿ ✿ ✿ ✿

CYCLING LOG

DATE	START TIME	END TIME

LOCATION

OBSERVATIONS

WEATHER _____

ROUTE _____
_____
_____
_____

DISTANCE _____

ELEVATION (gain/loss) _____

AVERAGE SPEED _____

DIFFICULTY   1   2   3   4   5   6   7   8   9   10

TERRAIN NOTES _____
_____
_____

EQUIPMENT NOTES _____
_____
_____

HIGHLIGHTS _____
_____
_____
_____

OVERALL RATING   ⚙ ⚙ ⚙ ⚙ ⚙

CYCLING LOG

LOG #

DATE

START TIME

END TIME

LOCATION

OBSERVATIONS

WEATHER _____

ROUTE _____
_____
_____
_____

DISTANCE _____

ELEVATION (gain/loss) _____

AVERAGE SPEED _____

DIFFICULTY   1   2   3   4   5   6   7   8   9   10

TERRAIN NOTES _____
_____
_____

EQUIPMENT NOTES _____
_____
_____

HIGHLIGHTS _____
_____
_____
_____

OVERALL RATING

CYCLING LOG

LOG #

DATE

START TIME

END TIME

LOCATION

OBSERVATIONS

WEATHER _____

ROUTE _____

_____

_____

_____

DISTANCE _____

ELEVATION (gain/loss) _____

AVERAGE SPEED _____

DIFFICULTY	1	2	3	4	5	6	7	8	9	10

TERRAIN NOTES _____

_____

_____

EQUIPMENT NOTES _____

_____

_____

HIGHLIGHTS _____

_____

_____

_____

_____

OVERALL RATING ✦ ✦ ✦ ✦ ✦

CYCLING LOG

LOG #

DATE	START TIME	END TIME

LOCATION

OBSERVATIONS

WEATHER _____

ROUTE _____
_____
_____
_____

DISTANCE _____

ELEVATION (gain/loss) _____

AVERAGE SPEED _____

DIFFICULTY	1	2	3	4	5	6	7	8	9	10

TERRAIN NOTES _____
_____
_____

EQUIPMENT NOTES _____
_____
_____

HIGHLIGHTS _____
_____
_____
_____

OVERALL RATING ⚙ ⚙ ⚙ ⚙ ⚙

CYCLING LOG

LOG #

DATE

START TIME

END TIME

LOCATION

OBSERVATIONS

WEATHER _____

ROUTE _____
_____
_____
_____

DISTANCE _____

ELEVATION (gain/loss) _____

AVERAGE SPEED _____

DIFFICULTY   1   2   3   4   5   6   7   8   9   10

TERRAIN NOTES _____
_____
_____

EQUIPMENT NOTES _____
_____
_____

HIGHLIGHTS _____
_____
_____
_____
_____

OVERALL RATING ✿ ✿ ✿ ✿ ✿

CYCLING LOG

LOG #

DATE

START TIME

END TIME

LOCATION

OBSERVATIONS

WEATHER _____

ROUTE _____
_____
_____
_____

DISTANCE _____

ELEVATION (gain/loss) _____

AVERAGE SPEED _____

DIFFICULTY	1	2	3	4	5	6	7	8	9	10

TERRAIN NOTES _____
_____
_____

EQUIPMENT NOTES _____
_____
_____

HIGHLIGHTS _____
_____
_____
_____

OVERALL RATING ⚙ ⚙ ⚙ ⚙ ⚙

CYCLING LOG

LOG #

DATE

START TIME

END TIME

LOCATION

OBSERVATIONS

WEATHER _____

ROUTE _____
_____
_____
_____

DISTANCE _____

ELEVATION (gain/loss) _____

AVERAGE SPEED _____

DIFFICULTY	1	2	3	4	5	6	7	8	9	10

TERRAIN NOTES _____
_____
_____

EQUIPMENT NOTES _____
_____
_____

HIGHLIGHTS _____
_____
_____
_____
_____

OVERALL RATING ⚙ ⚙ ⚙ ⚙ ⚙

CYCLING LOG

LOG #

DATE	START TIME	END TIME

LOCATION

OBSERVATIONS

WEATHER _____

ROUTE _____

_____

_____

_____

DISTANCE _____

ELEVATION (gain/loss) _____

AVERAGE SPEED _____

DIFFICULTY	1	2	3	4	5	6	7	8	9	10

TERRAIN NOTES _____

_____

_____

EQUIPMENT NOTES _____

_____

_____

HIGHLIGHTS _____

_____

_____

_____

_____

OVERALL RATING ⚙ ⚙ ⚙ ⚙ ⚙

CYCLING LOG

LOG #

DATE	START TIME	END TIME

LOCATION

OBSERVATIONS

WEATHER _____

ROUTE _____

_____

_____

_____

DISTANCE _____

ELEVATION (gain/loss) _____

AVERAGE SPEED _____

DIFFICULTY	1	2	3	4	5	6	7	8	9	10

TERRAIN NOTES _____

_____

_____

EQUIPMENT NOTES _____

_____

_____

HIGHLIGHTS _____

_____

_____

_____

_____

OVERALL RATING ⚙ ⚙ ⚙ ⚙ ⚙

CYCLING LOG

LOG #

DATE

START TIME

END TIME

LOCATION

OBSERVATIONS

WEATHER _____

ROUTE _____

_____

_____

_____

DISTANCE _____

ELEVATION (gain/loss) _____

AVERAGE SPEED _____

DIFFICULTY	1	2	3	4	5	6	7	8	9	10

TERRAIN NOTES _____

_____

_____

EQUIPMENT NOTES _____

_____

_____

HIGHLIGHTS _____

_____

_____

_____

_____

OVERALL RATING ⚙ ⚙ ⚙ ⚙ ⚙

CYCLING LOG

LOG #

DATE

START TIME

END TIME

LOCATION

OBSERVATIONS

WEATHER _____

ROUTE _____

_____

_____

_____

DISTANCE _____

ELEVATION (gain/loss) _____

AVERAGE SPEED _____

DIFFICULTY 1 2 3 4 5 6 7 8 9 10

TERRAIN NOTES _____

_____

_____

EQUIPMENT NOTES _____

_____

_____

HIGHLIGHTS _____

_____

_____

_____

OVERALL RATING ⚙ ⚙ ⚙ ⚙ ⚙

CYCLING LOG

LOG #

DATE	START TIME	END TIME

LOCATION

OBSERVATIONS

WEATHER _____

ROUTE _____

_____

_____

_____

DISTANCE _____

ELEVATION (gain/loss) _____

AVERAGE SPEED _____

DIFFICULTY	1	2	3	4	5	6	7	8	9	10

TERRAIN NOTES _____

_____

_____

EQUIPMENT NOTES _____

_____

_____

HIGHLIGHTS _____

_____

_____

_____

_____

OVERALL RATING ⚙ ⚙ ⚙ ⚙ ⚙

CYCLING LOG

LOG #

DATE

START TIME

END TIME

LOCATION

OBSERVATIONS

WEATHER _____

ROUTE _____

_____

_____

_____

DISTANCE _____

ELEVATION (gain/loss) _____

AVERAGE SPEED _____

DIFFICULTY   1   2   3   4   5   6   7   8   9   10

TERRAIN NOTES _____

_____

_____

EQUIPMENT NOTES _____

_____

_____

HIGHLIGHTS _____

_____

_____

_____

OVERALL RATING ⚙ ⚙ ⚙ ⚙ ⚙

CYCLING LOG

LOG #

DATE

START TIME

END TIME

LOCATION

OBSERVATIONS

WEATHER _____

ROUTE _____

_____

_____

_____

DISTANCE _____

ELEVATION (gain/loss) _____

AVERAGE SPEED _____

DIFFICULTY   1   2   3   4   5   6   7   8   9   10

TERRAIN NOTES _____

_____

_____

EQUIPMENT NOTES _____

_____

_____

HIGHLIGHTS _____

_____

_____

_____

_____

OVERALL RATING ⚙ ⚙ ⚙ ⚙ ⚙

CYCLING LOG

LOG #

DATE

START TIME

END TIME

LOCATION

OBSERVATIONS

WEATHER _____

ROUTE _____
_____
_____
_____

DISTANCE _____

ELEVATION (gain/loss) _____

AVERAGE SPEED _____

DIFFICULTY	1	2	3	4	5	6	7	8	9	10

TERRAIN NOTES _____
_____
_____

EQUIPMENT NOTES _____
_____
_____

HIGHLIGHTS _____
_____
_____
_____

OVERALL RATING ⚙ ⚙ ⚙ ⚙ ⚙

CYCLING LOG

LOG #

DATE

START TIME

END TIME

LOCATION

OBSERVATIONS

WEATHER _____

ROUTE _____

_____

_____

_____

DISTANCE _____

ELEVATION (gain/loss) _____

AVERAGE SPEED _____

DIFFICULTY	1	2	3	4	5	6	7	8	9	10

TERRAIN NOTES _____

_____

_____

EQUIPMENT NOTES _____

_____

_____

HIGHLIGHTS _____

_____

_____

_____

_____

OVERALL RATING   ✿ ✿ ✿ ✿ ✿

CYCLING LOG

LOG #

DATE

START TIME

END TIME

LOCATION

OBSERVATIONS

WEATHER _____

ROUTE _____

_____

_____

_____

DISTANCE _____

ELEVATION (gain/loss) _____

AVERAGE SPEED _____

| DIFFICULTY | 1 | 2 | 3 | 4 | 5 | 6 | 7 | 8 | 9 | 10 |

TERRAIN NOTES _____

_____

_____

EQUIPMENT NOTES _____

_____

_____

HIGHLIGHTS _____

_____

_____

_____

OVERALL RATING ⚙ ⚙ ⚙ ⚙ ⚙

CYCLING LOG

LOG #

DATE

START TIME

END TIME

LOCATION

OBSERVATIONS

WEATHER _____

ROUTE _____

_____

_____

_____

DISTANCE _____

ELEVATION (gain/loss) _____

AVERAGE SPEED _____

DIFFICULTY	1	2	3	4	5	6	7	8	9	10

TERRAIN NOTES _____

_____

_____

EQUIPMENT NOTES _____

_____

_____

HIGHLIGHTS _____

_____

_____

_____

_____

OVERALL RATING ⚙ ⚙ ⚙ ⚙ ⚙

NOTES & SKETCHES

"RIDE AS MUCH OR AS LITTLE, AS LONG OR
AS SHORT AS YOU FEEL. BUT RIDE."

—Eddy Merck

"YOU ARE ONE RIDE AWAY FROM A GOOD MOOD."

—Sara Bentley

"IT IS THE UNKNOWN AROUND THE CORNER
THAT TURNS MY WHEELS."
—Heinz Stücke

"LIFE IS LIKE RIDING A BICYCLE.
TO KEEP YOUR BALANCE YOU MUST KEEP MOVING."

—Albert Einstein

"WHEN MAN INVENTED THE BICYCLE HE REACHED
THE PEAK OF HIS ATTAINMENTS."
—Elizabeth West

"THE BICYCLE IS JUST AS GOOD COMPANY AS MOST HUSBANDS AND, WHEN IT GETS OLD AND SHABBY, A WOMAN CAN DISPOSE OF IT AND GET A NEW ONE WITHOUT SHOCKING THE ENTIRE COMMUNITY."

—Ann Strong

"CYCLISTS SEE CONSIDERABLY MORE OF THIS BEAUTIFUL WORLD
THAN ANY OTHER CLASS OF CITIZENS. A GOOD BICYCLE, WELL
APPLIED, WILL CURE MOST ILLS THIS FLESH IS HEIR TO."

—Dr. K. K. Doty

"IT NEVER GETS EASIER, YOU JUST GO FASTER."

—Greg LeMond

"WHEN THE SPIRITS ARE LOW, WHEN THE DAY APPEARS DARK,
WHEN WORK BECOMES MONOTONOUS, WHEN HOPE HARDLY
SEEMS WORTH HAVING, JUST MOUNT A BICYCLE AND GO OUT
FOR A SPIN DOWN THE ROAD, WITHOUT THOUGHT ON
ANYTHING BUT THE RIDE YOU ARE TAKING."

—Sir Arthur Conan Doyle

CYCLING CHECKLISTS

MY ALL-TIME FAVORITE CYCLING TRIPS

YOU'LL ALWAYS TREASURE those truly glorious days out on the bike. Keep track of your most memorable cycling trips here.

DATE

LOCATION

HIGHLIGHTS

DATE

LOCATION

HIGHLIGHTS

DATE **LOCATION**

HIGHLIGHTS

_____

_____

_____

_____

_____

_____

DATE **LOCATION**

HIGHLIGHTS

_____

_____

_____

_____

_____

_____

DATE **LOCATION**

HIGHLIGHTS

_____

_____

_____

_____

_____

_____

MY CYCLING BUCKET LIST

HERE'S WHERE YOU CAN GET AMBITIOUS: List the toughest trails, the highest peaks, and the fastest times you'd like to achieve. Check these goals off as you meet them, and add new ones as you dream bigger.

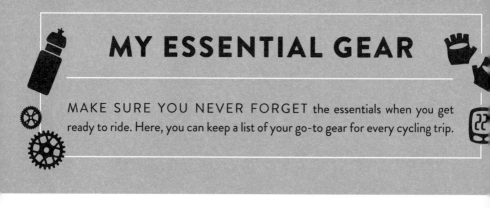

MY ESSENTIAL GEAR

MAKE SURE YOU NEVER FORGET the essentials when you get ready to ride. Here, you can keep a list of your go-to gear for every cycling trip.

- [ ] _____
- [ ] _____
- [ ] _____
- [ ] _____
- [ ] _____
- [ ] _____
- [ ] _____
- [ ] _____
- [ ] _____
- [ ] _____
- [ ] _____
- [ ] _____
- [ ] _____
- [ ] _____
- [ ] _____
- [ ] _____
- [ ] _____
- [ ] _____
- [ ] _____
- [ ] _____
- [ ] _____

MY MOST CHALLENGING ROUTES

KEEP A RUNNING LIST OF THE cycling routes that really pushed your limits, from your longest hauls to your highest elevations.

ROUTE	DATE	NOTES

MY MOST CHALLENGING ROUTES

ROUTE	DATE	LOCATION

BEST THINGS I'VE SEEN ON A BIKE

ON THESE PAGES, RECORD all the incredible sights you've seen from your bike: unusual creatures, amazing vistas, intense storms—anything that really made an impression.

SIGHT SEEN	DATE	LOCATION

BEST THINGS I'VE SEEN ON A BIKE

SIGHT SEEN	DATE	LOCATION

THE CYCLIST'S JOURNAL

weldon**owen**

www.weldonowen.com

ISBN: 978-1-68188-644-2

PRINTED IN CHINA

10 9 8 7 6 5 4 3 2 1

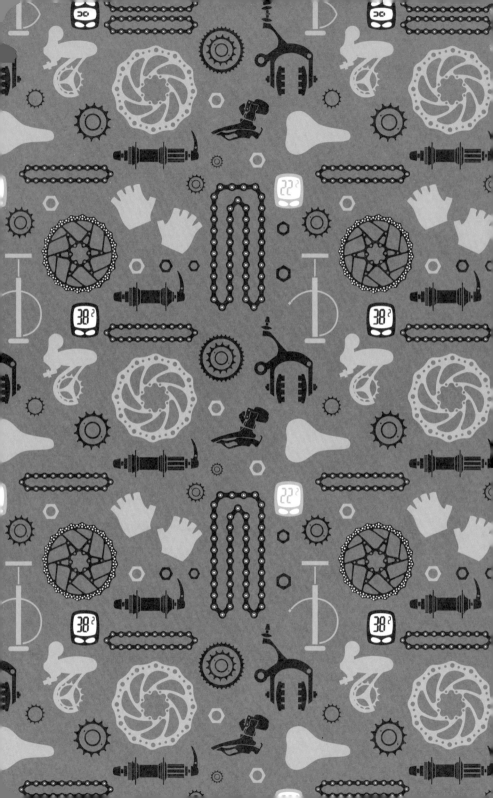